Taylor Made

My Journey to the NFL and Beyond

BY KERRY TAYLOR

Copyright © 2019 Kerry Taylor

ISBN: 9781089684077

The author disclaims responsibility for adverse effects or consequences from the misapplication or injudicious use of the information contained in this book. Mention of resources and associations does not imply an endorsement.

This book is dedicated to my daughter, Adrionna.

Thank you for indirectly giving me confidence to put myself out into the world. Remember, you can be anything you want to be in this world. Don't let anyone tell you otherwise. The road will be a tough one. Yell, cry, be frustrated, be angry but stay dedicated to yourself and what you want. You will get there. Daddy loves you!

Table of Contents

Foreword by Marc Megna 1

Introduction 5

Chapter 1: Don't Just Dream…Dream Big 13

Chapter 2: Get Laser-Focused and Prepared 21

Chapter 3: We Aren't in Kansas Anymore 27

Chapter 4: Game Time 35

Chapter 5: When One Door Closes 39

Chapter 6: Another One Opens 43

Chapter 7: Back in Friendly Confines 49

Chapter 8: New Sheriff in Town 53

Chapter 9: Roll With the Punches 57

Chapter 10: The Competition Increases 61

Chapter 11: The Grim Reaper Reappears 65

Chapter 12: Stay Ready 69

Chapter 13: Quit or Keep Pushing.................................73

Chapter 14: Let's Take It Inside.....................................77

Chapter 15: Can't Make the Club in the Tub................81

Chapter 16: Time to Take a Step Back and Regroup.....85

Chapter 17: The Rear View..93

Acknowledgements 99

Foreword

Iremember my redshirt freshman season on The University of Richmond Football team. We were on the road playing in our first game of the season. Our opponent was the University of Massachusetts. They were a powerful program loaded with great athletes. This was the first time I saw Kerry Taylor. He stood 6'2 and weighed in at 250 lbs. He already looked every bit of an NFL tight end. He was fast, athletic, and had great hands. He reminded me of a basketball player who lifted weights in the off-season. He was an absolute force to be reckoned with. Every year we would battle the Minutemen and it would be an absolute war. Sometimes they would top us and sometimes we would top them. Regardless of the outcome Kerry would be their primary target as a receiver. He dominated anyone trying to cover him. My entire collegiate career I only saw this once. There was no one who had the smooth athletic ability that he possessed. I studied all of our opponents and he always impressed our entire defensive unit. Every tight end I would come across would be compared to Kerry Taylor. Did they have all the necessary intangibles and have the complete package. I didn't know it then, but our paths would cross again soon after our college career came to an end.

After the NFL Draft that year and the dust settled we both ended up in the same place. In the office of New England Patriots Head of Personnel Bobby Grier. We knew each other well, but never officially met. Mr. Grier introduced us and we shook hands. A few things immediately stood out. His size, a friendly smile, and a firm handshake. That day we were both signed to the practice squad and had to work like maniacs just to hold onto our spots. 2 kids from Southeastern Massachusetts with a dream of playing for the New England Patriots. It was a surreal experience to say the least. After every practice we stayed after doing extra work and battling to the final whistle. This was an incredible scene. Picture this. Pete Caroll coaching Kerry on tight end play and NFL legend Andre Tippett coaching me up on Linebacker play. There was no part of this that was half speed. They were in our faces every play demanding our absolute best.

Every rep of every drill was all out. Kerry worked incredibly hard and he earned my respect by always giving relentless effort. It was rare to see someone with that type of speed and strength. This was the start of a very close friendship. We began spending time together outside of the facility. Dinners and going out in the city of Boston was always fun with Kerry. Sean Morey another practice squad kid from Southeastern Mass was became a close friend who we spent lots of time with. I felt at home with the both of them. They were blue-collar kids, who had dream, and the goal of making it in the NFL. We held each other accountable and were there for each other during the tough and uncertain times as an NFL rookie.

Sean organized an off-season training schedule with assistant strength coach Mike Morrisey at the Taunton YMCA. The speed and conditioning sessions were absolutely brutal. Particularly, because we would talk trash and didn't want to be outdone by each other. These training sessions pushed us to the limit and helped us develop a certain toughness that would help us for the rest of our lives. There was a certain drive in Kerry that was special. This drive would become the catalyst that would carry him to his calling in life. He has become a lifelong friend and confidant that I can always turn to. Over the years I've watched Kerry become a seasoned trainer, business owner, and lead an entire community of people to better health. He was clearly meant to help people and add great value to this world. His kind heart and genuine soul are gifts to this world and it's a better place because of him. I have no doubt he will continue to impact others in the most positive way for years to come.

Marc Megna

CO-Owner of Anatomy (Miami Beach, FL and Miami, FL)

Coach, Trainer and Athlete Performance and Fitness Model

Former NFL and CFL Linebacker and Defensive End

Played for the New England Patriots, New York Jets, Cincinnati Bengals, Barcelona Dragons, Berlin Thunder, Montreal Alouettes

Introduction

B efore we dive into this journey, I just wanted to say thank you for choosing to see what my journey was like. I hope this helps to shine a positive and motivating light on what a kid with a dream can accomplish when they refuse to give up.

Let's dive in!

I grew up in the city of Boston, mostly playing this great game on concrete, in between cars and marking the goal lines with light posts, trees and the curbs of the city streets. When I played my first game, I was hooked. I didn't know much about the game at that point in time, but as I learned more from my dad and uncles, I dreamed that one day I would play in the NFL.

Growing up in the city and going to a city school, I really didn't participate in organized sports like football. I mostly just ran track and did martial arts. It wasn't until we surprisingly moved into the suburbs when I was 12 that I discovered my athletic abilities. I say "surprisingly," because it came completely out of the blue. There was no talk about us moving anywhere, but this was the best decision my mother made for the course of my life. What I didn't know was that one day around Christmas time, my mother saw a news report that was very alarming to her. A young kid my age was jumped for his new sneakers and his Triple F.A.T. goose jacket (like I had) on his way home from school. The first thing my mother asked me after I walked in the door from school that day was, "Kerry, if someone wanted to take your jacket and sneakers from you, what would you do?"

Like a tough young man, proud chested, I answered, "Ma, you gave these to me. I'm not going to let anyone take these from me. I'm not a punk!" Little did I know that I had just sealed it, and we were on our way to Mansfield, Massachusetts, a town I never been to, let alone heard of.

As my mom said, "Oh, no. No one is going to hurt my baby over some damn clothes!" Thankfully, she decided to make the move, because that is when I discovered my athletic abilities. That one decision changed the course of my life forever. Thanks, Ma!

I continued to play tag and tackle football but when I joined my new school, everyone insisted that I play basketball. Of course, the joke was on them. I couldn't play a lick of basketball. I could run fairly fast and jump pretty high, but get the ball in the hoop? That wasn't happening. To my surprise, I made the team, and I improved over the years.

Then came time to play organized football with pads. That was a little bit easier to get used to, but I was definitely embarrassed by my mother on the first day of practice. I had no cleats, so I was practicing in sneakers. Finally, my mother showed up with my cleats. Part of me wished she hadn't.

I remember it like it was yesterday (cue the flashback music and ripples). I saw my mother's car pull up to park in the distance. I was finally going to be able to at least not slip and fall during practice anymore, and I was excited about that. I glanced down at everyone's feet displaying our school colors of green, black, and white on their cleats. I couldn't wait to put on my own pair so that I felt like I belonged. Finally, she was at the field, and I jogged over to change my footwear. I opened up the fresh, new box, and to my surprise—or maybe I shouldn't be surprised, because my mother knew nothing about football—my chin dropped as I slowly pulled out the orange and white cleats from the box. Yup! You read right. Orange and white! My feet stuck out amongst the crowd.

So that was an interesting start for the new kid on the first day. You know how that can go, especially in high school!

"I guess that's how they do it in the city, huh?" I heard one kid whisper under his breath, amongst the quiet laughs in the background.

"Kerry, those cleats are going to make you look faster than everyone else on the field!" said one coach.

Ha ha . . .

Hey, it is what it is, right? It happens to everyone at some point. Mine just happened to be my first day of practice. My feet were glowing orange amongst a sea of black and white cleats, rustling through the green grass of the football field. My mother meant well, and she did what she had to do to make sure her boy had some cleats to play in. We weren't on the high socioeconomic ladder, so to my mother, cleats were cleats. They did what they were supposed to do and that's all that mattered.

Over the years everything settled in, and I got comfortable with being a three-sport athlete. I played football, basketball and ran track. They all coincided with each other to help me be better at each sport. Football made me a lot more durable and tougher than most on the basketball court. Basketball helped me to be more agile on the football field, and track helped me to become faster and more explosive for the other two sports. When my high school career came to a close, I decided I would attend the University of Massachusetts at Amherst. In my early years I wanted to continue doing all three sports, but as you will read in these pages, I eventually chose football as my passion and, you guessed it, I went on to play in the NFL. I won't give away everything here (you'll have to read the book to get the whole story), but clearly, I enjoyed sports and all things connected with it

Fast forward a few years, and I decided to add an additional element to my career by becoming a trainer and coach. In 2009, I opened my own gym called 212 Health and Performance. Before you get the question out, no, I'm not from New York, and we are not located in New York. The name 212 Health and Performance was inspired by the premise of 212°, which states that at 211°, water is hot. At 212°, it boils. With boiling water, comes steam, and with steam, you can power a locomotive. To me that was powerful stuff, and it directly applied to life and fitness. With that small degree of change you can generate so much power.

I opened 212 because over the years, training and working out allowed me to achieve a lot of things in my life. It allowed me to reach the dreams that I had as a little boy. I wanted to harvest that and do the same for others in the world. I have an insane obsession with wanting to help others achieve what they want in life, whether it be as a coach at the gym or a coach on the field.

I have often been shy about telling people the level of football I achieved in my life.

Why?

I have no clue.

Perhaps it's because I wasn't anyone truly special in my eyes. I wasn't the big-name guy that anyone cared about. I was just the Average Joe. Who would want to hear my story and find interest in me?

However, through a conversation with a member at the gym and an old college friend, I decided to overcome my shyness and tell my story through a blog. A blog made sense because I figured it would help motivate my gym members further or even help their kids who may play sports. When I wrote my first blog post, it was received well by my members, and that helped me build up the confidence to continue to share my story. Eventually, people began to ask me whether I had ever thought about writing a book.

So, here we are with my career on these next pages. I hope my journey can help you believe that anything is possible if you are willing to sacrifice, work hard, and stay focused on your dream. There will be challenges and pitfalls along the way as you pursue your dreams, but those are the parts of the journey that make it all worth it.

Let me set my story up for you before you head into Chapter 1.

The spring happens to be a great time of year for a football fan because it's when the NFL Draft happens. For a fan, it is all about seeing if your favorite team is going to draft the right players to get the team to the Super Bowl. Leading up to the draft, you are inundated by the media with information on what college player each team should draft. The experts spend months trying to predict what's going to happen at the draft. Even though they get some of it right, they never get it 100% correct. While all of this is going on, you have the college football player who has now realized that he may be able to make his childhood dream come true. All he did was work, work, work to give himself the best opportunity to have his name called on draft day. Of course, every player has a different journey with the draft and NFL.

Here is mine.

CHAPTER 1

Don't Just Dream ... Dream Big!

3, 2, 1 ... My senior year concluded, and we completed what most said was impossible. We won the Division 1 AA National Championship after finishing the previous season two and nine. I think my teammates and I celebrated that achievement for the whole second semester in college. With the conclusion to the season, there was also another impossible event that could happen. I had a shot at making my childhood dream come true. I could get drafted into the NFL.

The first time I was told that was by an NFL scout who was at school to sit and meet with me. I was very shocked and surprised. You see, my co-captain, Khari Samuel, was the one on our team that we knew was going to get an opportunity to play in the NFL. When NFL scouts came to see me, I thought it was a mistake. We had similar names and were both captains of the team. His name was Khari, my name is Kerry, so I assumed that was what had happened. But sure enough, it was me they wanted to see. We sat down and talked for roughly ten to fifteen minutes. The main point of the meeting was to let me know that they had interest in me being a part of their organization down the road, and they would be in contact in the future. That short conversation gave me the motivation I needed to get even more laser-focused on being the best overall athlete I could be.

Job number one was to identify an agent to help me through this process. Picking an agent was a tricky process. These guys are all trained talkers and salesmen. I wasn't sure who would put my best interest first. I would hear stories about agents not always doing right by the athlete. After talking with many agencies and having the boss, my mother, speak with all of them, we decided to go with an agency out of New York, Sports Stars, Inc. That's when I started to receive information on where I was predicted to get drafted, the workout numbers I should be putting up, what teams were interested in me and for what position, along with a laundry list of other information.

Unfortunately, I was not invited to the Combine that year or invited to play in any of the college all-star games, so I had to make sure I performed well at my Pro Days when

I had them. The first Pro Day I had was in front of scouts from the Green Bay Packers, Detroit Lions, Baltimore Ravens, Jacksonville Jaguars and the San Francisco 49ers.

A Pro Day, for those who are not familiar, is when you get tested in many different physical categories, then put through different football position-specific drills. You get interviewed by the different teams and have to take your Wonderlic test. I was extremely nervous when this day came. It was time to show what I had been doing the past few months and if I physically had what it took to play at the next level by the numbers.

In my mind I was thinking, "Here goes nothing!"

First up was the bench press, 225 x 27 reps; then the vertical jump, 34"; broad jump, 9'8"; and the forty-yard dash, 4.58. We continued with the three-cone drill, the twenty-yard shuttle run, and sixty-yard shuttle run.

Following that, we moved on to the skill portion of the workout. I was put through drills for a tight end, which was my natural position, but I was also put through drills as if I was an H-Back, also known as the move guy or flexed guy. Even though I was a tight end on our roster, the H-Back position fit more of what I did and my skill set. The H-Back is more of a jack-of-all-trades. It is a combination of tight end, full back, slot receiver, and wide receiver. These positions are what you see tight ends doing a lot of in the NFL today. I felt that my performance went well. The following week, the New England Patriots, Miami Dolphins and the Pittsburgh Steelers came to see what I had. I was put through the same testing in the weight room, but with better results. The on-the-field drills were a little bit different, as every team had a set of drills that they wanted you to perform to showcase your skills. I felt I performed well on those also.

After the teams left, it was a waiting game. There were many calls and discussions with my agent as to what to expect and what was going on. He mentioned that the Lions and Patriots wanted to bring me in for a visit to their facilities. I headed out to visit both places, and I had a great time meeting some of the players, coaches and seeing the facilities. I could definitely picture myself making one of these places my home for the next few years of my life, but would it come to be?

I waited and waited to hear the news. With the draft about a week away, my agent suggested that the earliest I could go would be the fifth round, which was fine with me as long as I got an opportunity.

Eventually the big day arrived—Draft Day. Back then it was only a two-day event, not the three-day event you see now. I watched the draft at home with my mother, little brother, and one of my college buddies. Let me tell you, it was one of the most stressful experiences I had ever been through in my life up to that point, but it was all for a good reason. I would be moving on to the next level and living my childhood dream, I hoped, fingers crossed. I know you may be saying, what could be so stressful? It was stressful because both days were filled with constant questions from family and friends, constant phone calls from friends and teammates asking whether I got drafted yet. The phone calls were the most stressful because that is how you find out if a team is picking you or not. Every time someone called my phone, I got my hopes up that it was a team calling me.

Day one came and went. I was not picked, but that was okay, I didn't expect to be a first day selection. If I was going to get drafted, it was going to be on day two.

Day two started out, and I began to see names of people I knew who I either played with or competed against. My teammate and fellow captain, Khari, who I mentioned earlier, was drafted by the Chicago Bears in the fifth round. My phone started ringing in the sixth round, but mostly for teams to tell me that they were thinking of taking me or another player with their next pick. That next pick would come and go, and I was still waiting. Then it was the Patriots' seventh-round pick.

The phone rang.

Could it be?

Yes! It was the New England Patriots, but just to let me know they were choosing between me and another player. The card was in and . . . the other player was chosen. Then it was the Lions' pick. My phone rang again. They said the same thing. The card was in and . . . the other player was chosen. Seven long rounds and 253 picks later, I was not selected.

I was disappointed, sad, and frustration set in. I didn't want to be bothered by anyone. A few minutes went by, and before I could fall deeper into my own personal pit of despair, my phone rang. It was my agent telling me that a few teams would like to sign me as a free agent. After going back and forth for a while with different teams, I agreed to become a Detroit Lion. It seemed as if my teammates were on the same call, because not ten minutes later, a few of them showed up at my house to pick me up and take me back to school to celebrate.

And celebrate we did! But that's a story for another day.

Now that I knew I would have an opportunity, there was no sitting back and relaxing. This only meant the door had been opened. I had not yet arrived in the NFL. It was time to hone my craft and show what I could really do once I got to mini-camp.

And that, folks, was my journey through the draft! If you have never seen the NFL draft, take a few minutes and check it out the next time it happens. If you decide to check it out, look at it from a college athlete's point of view, with all the emotions that those kids may be experiencing. It's a roller coaster ride, for sure.

CHAPTER 2
Get Laser-Focused and Prepared

After all the celebrating was done, and we recovered, it was time to get back to work. The first hurdle to make an NFL team was mini-camp in Detroit. I had to report in about three weeks, so I focused on staying in shape and doing all the football drills I could to get myself ready. I also had to make sure I was finishing up school strong and getting ready for graduation. Balancing the two wasn't really that difficult, but I made it very difficult on myself because I never thought I did enough each day to prepare myself for mini-camp. I mean, reality started to set in that I would be running routes against, and blocking, some of the best in the business.

Fortunately, the three weeks flew by, and soon enough it was time to head out for a weekend mini-camp in

Detroit, Michigan. As I arrived at the airport to head there, nervousness instantly overcame me. Every question I could ask myself ran through my mind. Did I do enough? Am I fast enough? Am I big enough? Is this really happening to me? It was a mentally-draining flight.

When I finally arrived in Detroit, it was time to meet some of my potential future teammates. As we all climbed into the shuttle to go to the Pontiac Silverdome, I was able to let out a sigh of relief. By looking at the eyes of some of the other players, you could see all the emotions flowing through them. Some felt the same way I did. Some had confidence. Some felt lost and others were cocky, like their stuff didn't stink. Together, we made the hour-long trek to the stadium, exchanging our college stories along the way.

When we arrived, we headed in to see the trainers and get checked out. Then we were given the playbook. Oh yes, the playbook! This monstrosity of information was three times the size of my college playbook. On top of that, I had to pick up our special teams playbook. Really? A special teams playbook? Things were clearly about to be very different!

Those two playbooks were about to become my two best friends, and I started right in. We had to be on the field in a few hours, so I had to study what was going to be going on at practice that day. Initially, my head was spinning. I mean, the playbook was huge, and I also had to decipher between old terminology and new terminology. For example, what we called Rip in college pertained to a formation. For the Lions, it was a motion and there were pages upon pages of this to go through.

The initial practice was tough, but we all got through it. I like to believe I had a pretty good first couple of days. In fact, everything went well until the last day.

The practice field had recently been renovated to put a sprinkler system in. One of the last plays that we practiced before we headed back into meetings was a pass play where I had to run a flag route, also known as a corner route. Basically, I ran down the field for eight-twelve yards and then broke on a forty-five-degree angle towards the pylon.

Well, . . .

The great thing was the ball was thrown to me, and I caught it. The bad thing was that I landed in a hole that was not fully refilled yet and ended up severely spraining my ankle. Thank God it happened at the end and not the beginning, because then I would have missed out on my opportunities to show what I could do. How bad was it? Well I needed crutches and had to be off if for about 2 weeks.

As mini-camp came to a close, it was time to head back to school for graduation. I would report back a few weeks later for training camp.

Graduation went well and flew by. Before I knew it, it was time to pack up and make my voyage back to Detroit to try to make the team. The hurdles I had to go through to get back were tough. I was still using an electric stim machine on my ankle, which ended up causing an issue at the airport. I had a battery pack with different knobs on it on my hip with different wires coming out of it leading down to my ankle with electrodes on the other end. This machine would send a constant flow of electric pulses to my ankle to promote healing. When I was checking in at security, they weren't having it. Even though I explained what it was for (you can picture me and about 5 airport security guards trying to figure out what it was, and me begging and pleading with them to just let me get on my flight), I was detained just long enough for me to miss my flight to Detroit. And, of course, there were no more flights out that day to make it there, so I had to wait until the next morning to catch a flight. Needless to say airport chairs and floors aren't the most comfortable things in the world.

When I finally got there, it was time to get to work. We had three days of rookie practices and then all the veterans showed up to get ready for the season. I was about to practice with and against some great players in the NFL. Because they aren't the New England Patriots, or on one of the top tier teams in the NFL, you may not know who they are, but let me share, anyway. I had to block two All-Pros—Robert

Porcher and Stephen Boyd, and also Allen Aldridge. The one thing I didn't get to do was block for Barry Sanders because he ended up retiring that year before training camp. I did meet him, for those of you who are wondering. After the media circus died down from that event, we had two practices at the Silverdome and then headed out to Saginaw, Michigan for training camp—or maybe I should just say that we headed to the corn fields.

You hear a ton of crazy things about training camp but are never sure what is the truth and what isn't. I was about to find out. If you would like to know what training camp was like, keep reading.

CHAPTER 3

We Aren't in Kansas Anymore

Thanks for turning the page.

This was another one-plus hour bus ride to Saginaw State University. I asked one of the guys, "Is anything close around here?"

He laughed and answered, "No!"

We did finally arrive, and it was time to check in and get our room key and golf cart key. Well, at least I thought I was getting a golf cart key. I guess I had my selective hearing ears on when they mentioned they were only for the veterans during training camp.

After getting our key and unpacking, we had to head to our first meeting of training camp. Starting back at the bottom of the totem pole is not going to be fun.

Our first team meeting was filled with expectations of the team during the season and training camp. Then, we watched some game film and had our special teams meeting. Special teams are the third phase of the game that usually involves the kicker. It consists of kickoff, kickoff return, punt, punt return, PAT and field goal. Special teams can have a huge impact on the outcome of a football game. The meeting, needless to say, lasted a while as we reviewed each team and the responsibilities of each person. If you're a rookie and have any hope of making an NFL roster, this is where you must make your impact. Terrell Davis, the Denver Bronco and Georgia Bulldog legend, made a huge hit on a kickoff. Up to that point he wasn't getting a chance to see the field at all. That one play and hit got him noticed and eventually catapulted a career that landed him in the NFL Hall of Fame. If you can't contribute on special teams, consider your chances gone. So, time to focus up and learn.

When the meeting was over, it was time to head to bed and try to rest. As a rookie, your day started a little bit earlier than the veterans. The following would be a typical day for me at training camp:

- 4:45 a.m.: Wake up

- 5:30 a.m.: Get taped by trainer (We had to be done before the veterans came in.)

- 6:00 a.m.: Breakfast/Workout

- 8:00 a.m.: Special teams meeting followed by team meeting, offensive/defensive meeting and then position meetings

- 10:00 a.m.: Practice

- 12:30 p.m.: Lunch/ Workout

- 1:00 p.m.: Break

- 3:00 p.m.: Taped

- 4:00 p.m.: Practice

- 6:30 p.m.: Dinner

- 8:00 p.m.: Meetings (same break down as the morning)

- 11:00 p.m.: Snack

- 11:30 p.m.: Bedtime

I don't want to bore you with the repetition and monotony that is training camp. What I will do is highlight some of the things that happened during that time that stick out in my mind.

High School Coach Visits

During the second week of training camp, the head coach of my high school football team, Mike Redding, came out to visit me for two days. It was great to see the coach who helped get my football career going and got me to this point. It was also great to see a familiar face from home at that point in time. Training camp had started to wear on me a bit, and to have one of my biggest supporters there to see me definitely recharged my batteries. A coach who believes in you is sometimes all you need to be successful and reach levels you never thought you could.

Rookie Song

Throughout training camp, every rookie or new guy to the team had to stand up on the table during one of the meals in the day and sing a song. It could be your school's fight song or anything you chose. The secret was to pick something that you knew most of the words to, but also make it a song that everyone would know. Why? Because the rest of the team will join in, and you won't have to sing as long. Plus you're not booed off the stage and told you have to go again before camp is over.

Can you guess what my song choice was?

"Alright, stop what you're doing cause I'm about to ruin the image and the style that you're used to."

You guessed it, the Humpty Dance! As soon as I started in, the rest of the team joined me. Great choice, if I do say so myself.

Talent Show

When we started training camp, I was in a group that re-enacted the retirement of Barry Sanders. We all re-enacted what we thought the coaches' reactions would've been when they first heard the news. Some people's opinion is that Barry was the greatest running back ever in the NFL. So, you can only imagine what the reactions were. It was pretty hilarious.

My Best Catch During Training Camp

This happened when my high school coach was up visiting me. We were having an intra-squad red-zone scrimmage. I think I did well in the scrimmage, but one of my highlights was an end-zone catch for a touchdown. I lined up on the right-hand side and ran a fifteen-yard choice hook route. That means I ran fifteen yards down field and, depending on the coverage, I either turned in or out. In my case, I turned in and shuffled away from the linebacker that was covering me. I saw the ball coming. It was thrown a little high, but I still gave it a shot. I just jumped as high as I could and hoped for the best. I was able to just barely reach it, clutch it, and come down with it. I was able to drag both my feet and get them in at the back of the end zone before the linebacker pushed me out of bounds. I shocked myself with the catch, but when you don't think about what you're doing on the field, your true athlete comes out. Funny thing was, when I got back to the huddle, the quarterback said, "Great job, man, but I was trying to throw it away!"

Massage Day and Worst Day of Practice Ever

Every Wednesday we had a massage school that came to give us massages. It was not a bad deal at all. The students got to practice, and they had a bunch of willing and able bodies. On this particular day, I was able to be double-teamed and really get the kinks worked out. They tenderized my body for about two hours. When I was done, it was time to get changed up and head out to practice. It started just like any other practice for me, but about twenty minutes into it, I started to get enormous aches and pains in every joint of my body. I couldn't run or move. Basically, I got my ass kicked all practice long. Come to find out, I forgot to drink fluids, which is especially important after having a massage. The toxins that were released into my system were wreaking havoc. Consider it a lesson learned on my part. Needless to say, I drank a small pond's worth of water throughout the rest of the day.

That is a quick summary of my training camp experience. When training camp officially broke, we headed back to Pontiac to continue to work together as a team and get ready for our pre-season games. First up was the Atlanta Falcons in Atlanta, Georgia.

How would I fare? Hmm . . . you'll have to find out in the next chapter!

In the meantime, keep striving to be a little bit better today than you were yesterday.

CHAPTER 4
Game Time

The time had finally come. It was game prep for our first preseason game against the Dirty Birds! The best thing about this trip was that I'd be able to see my father and his family. Knowing that gave me a sense of relaxation and not the usual tremors of butterflies I had been feeling each time I took the field. It also allowed me to have even more excitement about my FIRST NFL GAME!

We arrived at the stadium around 4 p.m. for a 7 p.m. game. I started to go through my usual pre-game routine. Every athlete has a routine. Mine was pretty simple. I would spend about ten minutes stretching myself out while listening to calypso music. Then, off to the training room to get my ankles and wrist taped up. Once that was completed, I headed out to the field, and shifted my music over to

DMX. With each step forward, the lights got brighter and brighter as I journeyed down the tunnel to the field. It was my first time in a dome for game day. To see everything that goes on behind the scenes was an amazing sight. After the awesomeness of what was going on wore off, I continued with my routine. I went through numerous run-blocking and catching drills. My mission was to catch a total of 100 balls. The 100th ball was caught, and back into the locker room I went to get ready for team drills and pre-game.

Finally, it was time for the game to start. My adrenaline was high, and my excitement level was through the roof, but I had to wait my turn to get some live action on the field. I stood on the sidelines and looked around for my dad. I was able to spot him. He was up in the upper deck, and I waved excitedly and refocused on the game. The first quarter came to a close, and finally it was my time. "Kerry, go in with the second group at tight end," yelled my coach.

My first play ever in a live NFL game ended up being a play-action pass. We broke the huddle and hustled to the line of scrimmage. As I lined up and placed my hand on the ground, I looked up. Lined up right across from me was the Falcon's number one draft pick that year, Patrick Kerney. It was no big deal, at least not on this play, anyway. The quarterback bellowed out the cadence and finished with an assertive shout of "Hike!" I kept running towards the sideline to get open. The QB and I made eye contact.

That's when I realized the ball was about to be launched my way. The QB cocked his arm back and then everything slowed down as the ball took flight. It seemed like it took forever before I snatched it out of the air and clutched onto it for dear life. Once it was secured, I turned upfield. Out of the corner of my right eye, I saw two defenders coming to tackle me. Then I came up with the genius idea that I was going to hurdle them, so airborne I went.

Boy, was I wrong! One guy went high and the other went low, and I was driven out of bounds. Wahoo! You have no idea how good it felt at that moment. I wish I could've stopped time for that moment just a little longer. I had one more catch in this series and then the drive stalled. As I jogged to the sideline, I heard my name being yelled out loud. As I looked around, lo and behold, it was my dad. Somehow my dad, sister and family made their way down to the second row. To see the excitement on their faces was priceless. In the next series, I was able to show that my skills as a run blocker had improved. I wasn't as big or long as some of the other guys, so my technique had to be flawless. I'm proud to say their first-round draft pick did not make any tackles when he was my blocking assignment. When the game was over, I ended up with four catches for roughly 75 yards. I wish I could've done more in that game, but I felt I proved I could catch, get open and block. Unfortunately, we lost the game, but it was a win for me internally, because I proved to myself that I could hang with the big boys.

The rest of the preseason did not work out the way we wanted. We lost all our preseason games. I like to believe I personally ended up with a pretty good preseason, but, as our last preseason game against the Dolphins ended, my attention was redirected. Up to this point, I had made it through every cut. However, there was still one more to go.

Would I make Detroit my home for the season?

Keep reading to see what happened when I sat down with the Head Coach, Bobby Ross!

CHAPTER 5

When One Door Closes

Up until now you have been able to have an inside look at what an aspiring NFL football player goes through—my own personal "hard knocks," so to speak.

Every story has its peaks and valleys. I felt I was at a peak and on cloud 9 for the next few days. My story with the Detroit Lions accumulates to these next few days. I have always been the type who kept my head down and worked hard for what I wanted. I would come up for air when I finally got to where I wanted to be. Well, it was time to come up for air a little bit.

We had the next few days off. I felt, up to this point, that I had done enough to make the team, so I did something that was very uncharacteristic of me; I ventured around the area to see what there was out there for places to live. That's how confident I was in how I performed in training camp, practices, games and just all around. I figured I would at least make practice squad.

Those three days went by in a snap. Feeling confident and good about myself, I headed back to the Silverdome for our first official regular season game practice. I walked into the locker room to get myself changed up for practice and a sudden uneasiness came over me. Ladies and gentlemen, this is where I met the Reaper.

This is the guy on staff who is in charge of telling the players to grab their playbook so they could meet the coach. And here it was. "Hey, Kerry, Coach Ross would like to meet with you. Please bring your playbook."

The key part to that sentence I later found out was, "bring your playbook." I remember the rest of this moment like it was yesterday (key the dramatic flashback effect). I took a seat in a large brown leather chair across from Coach Ross who was sitting behind an enormous dark brown oak desk with different trophies, awards, and plaques on the wall behind him. Even with all that, there was one part of his desk that immediately caught my eye. It was the stack of powder blue playbooks that stood about four feet high, and on these playbooks were the names of some of the players I had become good friends with over our time together. That's when I started to get the feeling that this was the end of the road for me. Still, deep down inside,

I was holding on tightly to HOPE. Internally I thought maybe he was taking everyone's playbook and giving some of us our game week playbook.

Ahh, but I digress, because unfortunately, the inevitable happened. I knew it was coming from the first words out of his mouth. "Kerry, you had a helluva camp, and you should be in the NFL for a long time with your skill set . . ." At that point everything else sounded like the teacher from Charlie Brown.

And here it comes. ". . . but we are only going to keep three tight ends on our roster this season. I would like to keep the three veterans we have. But if you clear waivers, we may try to keep you here for our practice squad."

As crushed and disappointed as I was, all I could say was, "Thank you, Coach, for the opportunity. I truly enjoyed the challenge. Best of luck to you this year." I tried to give him one of the firmest handshakes I have ever given to someone, turned around and walked out of the room. I tried to walk around with my head held high, but at that moment the floor seemed to be the only thing worth looking at.

I headed into the locker room, packed up my personal belongings, and exchanged numbers with some of the veterans who I had become friends with over the last six months. I took time to thank all of the other team personnel. I grabbed my flight info and headed out of the stadium to catch the shuttle back to my hotel room to pack. Just before I got on the shuttle, two of the veterans in my tight end group said, "Keep your head up. It's a business at the end of the day. You have nothing to be ashamed of. Keep working. Someone will pick you up."

I dragged my feet onto the shuttle and headed back to the hotel. My thoughts and mind were all over the place. "NOW WHAT?!" I kicked my room door open and plopped onto the bed for a minute, staring at the ceiling. Then, to my amazement, the phone rang. For a moment I had a rush of excitement, but it quickly disappeared because I was feeling really sorry for myself. At that point in time, I didn't feel like speaking to anyone. I thought it was probably just my mom or uncle calling, and so I didn't answer. Two minutes later, it rang again. This time, I took a deep breath and got ready to explain to my family what had happened.

I picked up the phone, and on the other end the voice said, "Kerry, how are you feeling?"

Can you guess whose voice was on the other end? Was it my mother? Uncle? Other teammates that were going through the same thing? The Lions calling me back? My agent? A new team? The front desk of the hotel? You'll have to read the next chapter to find out who was on the phone.

Until then, continue to live a life one degree above the rest.

CHAPTER 6
Another One Opens

M e: "I've had better days, but I'm doing good."
Person: "What time is your flight home?"

Me: "Three thirty this afternoon, I should land around seven tonight at Logan."

Person: "Okay, great. Use this flight to put everything behind you. I will need you with a clear head tomorrow."

Me: "Okay. No problem. By the way, who is this?"

Person: "Oh, that would probably help you out, wouldn't it? This is Carl Smith, Tight End Coach for the New England Patriots."

Me: "Hey, Coach!"

Coach Smith: "We would like you to come down to the stadium tomorrow and sign a contract. Would you like to be a New England Patriot?"

Me: "Of course I would, Coach. I'll come down as soon as I get off the plane, if you would like!"

Coach Smith: "Ha ha, tomorrow's fine. See you then."

Me: "Okay. Great, Coach! I'm looking forward to it!"

And just like that, my hope was instantly renewed. My excitement that this dream was not over couldn't be contained. Constant pacing around the room and self-conversations ensued as I hung up the phone. *Yes, I'm gonna make this happen!! Learn from your past mistakes, Kerry. We have to work even harder to make this happen.* These were some of the words I started speaking out loud to myself. Then I stopped in my tracks, jumped on the bed and did the happy dance. *I'm going to be a New England Patriot! Yeah, Boy!*

After my five minutes of celebrating with myself, I remembered I had to pack up all my belongings and head to the airport. I don't think you ever saw a person pack a bag so fast. When I landed back home, my smile quickly changed into a slight frown. I know my mom means well, but all I could picture was the long ride home having to answer questions as to why I didn't make the team and then explaining how I have an opportunity to be with the home team New England Patriots.

Side Bar:

To show you how much my mother knows about football, during a game in college, I was called for a holding penalty. "Holding, #88." All of the sudden a loud yell that only a proud mother could make came from the stands. "That's my baby! Keep it up!" My teammates all came over to me laughing and smiling. "Kerry, does she know that's not a good thing?" Or better yet, after we scored a touchdown in a game, I looked at the fence behind the bench and my mother was standing there with a very concerned and pissed off look on her face, so I got up and walked over to her. "Hey, ma, what's up?" I asked. "Why are you playing the whole game. Why aren't they giving you a rest? I'm going to have a talk with your coach after the game. They aren't going to just use my baby," she responded in only a way a concerned mother would! But I had to quickly correct her, "Ma, it's a great thing that I'm not getting a rest. That means I'm playing. That means I'm good at what I do. If I'm not playing and sitting all the time, that's not a good thing. Go enjoy the rest of the game." She responded with a smile, laughed, apologized and went back to her seat. My teammates still get a kick out of that one.

Love you, Ma.

Needless to say, I didn't sleep that night. The next day, I headed over to what was then called Foxboro Stadium. When I walked in, I was brought down to the offices to go over the details of my contract and get that signed. Once the contract was signed, I was shown to my locker and given a quick tour of the stadium. On my tour, I bumped into a soon-to-be great friend, Marc Megna. Marc and I played against each other all through college. He's a Fall River native, but neither one of us knew each other until this point. I also realized that I would be meeting Sean Morey, another native of Massachusetts by way of Marshfield, who played for my former head coach, Mark Whipple, at Brown University. I heard so much about him from watching film as I had to learn a new offense that featured him as the go to receiver. Little did I know, Marc and Sean would become two great friends of mine throughout my career and life. We all had the same mentality of giving our all and never quitting. After the tour, I headed home and was ready to get things going. Of course, I had another sleepless night.

The next day, I began my journey as a New England Patriot. I was going to learn from one of the best tight ends in the game at that point in time, Ben Coates! Hot dog! (Sorry for the Mickey Mouse Club reference) The first day was a tough one for me, though. Contrary to what many may think, I'm a very shy and quiet person. I had to get reacquainted quickly so I could feel comfortable and be myself on the field. The days that followed looked like this:

- **5 a.m.**: Wake up

- **6:30 a.m.**: Arrive at stadium

- **7 a.m.**: Workout

- **8:30 a.m.**: Breakfast

- **9 a.m.**: Team meeting

- **9:30 a.m.**: Offensive group meeting

- **10:15 a.m.**: Position meetings

- **11 a.m.**: Special teams meeting

- **12 p.m.**: Lunch

- **2 p.m.-4 p.m.**: Practice

- **4:30 p.m.**: Team meeting

- **5 p.m.**: Offensive group meeting

- **6:30 p.m.**: Home

They were long days, but I loved every bit of it. This season was filled with its ups and down, just like every season, but my goal was to have a lot more ups than downs. Curious to what those roller coaster moments were? Turn the page and read on as I share my experiences throughout the season.

Until next time, continue to live a life 1° above the rest.

CHAPTER 7

Back in Friendly Confines

Ah, man, it's great to be back at home! My season with the Patriots was filled with a ton of new experiences and adventures. Here is a quick look into some of them.

Practice After Practice

Yes, we talkin' 'bout practice! (In my Allen Iverson voice). I mentioned to you in the previous chapter about bumping into my friend, Marc, on the tour of the stadium. Marc and I play opposing positions. Up to this point, I never had to block him or run routes against him. In college, he was one of the greatest interior defensive linemen to put on a Richmond Spiders' uniform. In the NFL, he was moved to outside linebacker. One day after practice, we were walking off the field when Coach Carroll called us both back over.

"Alright, let's see you guys get after it!" We threw our pads back on and banged heads for another ten-fifteen minutes. This happened at least two times every week. I didn't mind it at all. The more reps, the better. For both of us, every snap was a battle. Once we were across from each other with helmets on, the friendship went out the window. With each collision, sweat and spit flew everywhere until the whistle blew. We took twenty seconds and crashed into each other again, all under the watchful eye of Coach Carroll and our position coaches and some vets. Talk about pressure to perform! All eyes on you! That meant neither one of us blue collar workers was going to give even a little. We both had the same mindset of never giving up and pushing ourselves to the limit, so you could imagine how this went. I would have to say that the result of all the battles was a draw!

Getting Threatened by Big Willie

In practice, I often lined up across from two Pro Bowl players, Willie (McGinest) and Chris (Slade). My task was to block them. Who gets that lucky every day? On this day I had to reach block Willie to allow our running back to get around the corner, and I wasn't the type of player to take a play off and go half speed. I was young, hungry and trying to keep a job. You may be already jumping ahead to the idea of what happened.

I approached the line, and Willie wasn't fully strapped up. I successfully achieved my block so the running back could get around the corner and run for thirty yards. As I walked back to the huddle to the crowd of players and coaches telling me, "Great job," Willie's voice bellowed over the crowd as he approached me with a little pep in his step. He got right in my face and said, "Hey, rookie, don't you ever do that again!" I turned and got back into the huddle. "Great job, Kerry, that's how you stick around in this league," and then (I saw it coming), "Run the same play, Kerry. Do the same thing." We broke the huddle, and I lined up across from Willie again. But this time his helmet was fully strapped, hands balled up and clenched tightly, ready to go with continuous expletives flying out of his mouth. "HIKE!" Suddenly everything went in slow motion as we banged heads. I felt all eyes on me. I am happy to say I successfully completed my block again to achieve the same result. Chalk one up for the little new guy.

Promoted to a Starter

Well, not really. During the season—I think it was week nine—Big Ben was a little banged up, so I rotated in with the starters during the week for practice. My excitement was through the roof. When game time came, Ben was healthy and ready to go. So, back to the bottom of the list I went. Take a seat, rookie!

The Announcement

The day came when Coach Carroll was fired, and Coach Belichick was hired. It was an exciting day for many, but a very disappointing day for me.

"Why," you ask?

Because Coach Carroll and his coaching staff gave me a chance. He took a shot on me. I was excited to eventually pay him back with my play on the field. Not only that, but I spent the past year proving that the coach made the right decision and then, boom, he was gone. Out with the old staff, in with the new staff, is often the way with sports teams. Where did this leave your little-known, undersized rookie tight end from UMass Amherst? Hmm . . .

Keep reading, because in Chapter 8 I will fill you in.

Until then, continue to live a life 1° above everyone else.

CHAPTER 8
New Sheriff in Town

The announcement was one for the sports history books. The hiring of Bill Belichick and the firing of Pete Carroll severely impacted the landscape of the NFL. Still, to this day, you see the effects of it. These two coaches were two of the best coaches in the NFL. You wouldn't have thought back then that, combined, they would be a part of the playoffs for the next sixteen of nineteen years and be a part of ten of the last nineteen Super Bowls. This change also affected my career as well. Coach Carroll believed in me and brought me here. Now what?

Sitting in the meeting room with the rest of the team, I didn't know how to feel or what to expect. All I knew was we were getting a new head coach, and I was back at square one. In order to get to where I wanted, I was going to have to get acclimated as quickly as possible. After Coach Carroll said his goodbyes, Coach Belichick entered the meeting room. Most of the veterans were excited for the change. As a rookie, I just followed suit. Here are some of the first words out of Coach Belichick's mouth as I remember them, in his non-emotional, intense, calm demeanor.

"Okay, guys, I'm happy to be here. Let's just get a few things straight. No one is above the team. No one! Everything stays amongst the people in this room. If you're interviewed, give them simple, non-exploratory answers. If someone gets hurt and you're asked about it, you answer, "They are doing just fine," "No comment," or "We're working hard to be ready for next week." Remember, we are a team and that's how we will conduct ourselves. None of this other bullshit you see on TV."

After the meeting, some of us immediately had to schedule meetings with our position coaches. In that meeting I was told I had a lot of potential, and I would be with the development group up until training camp. That meant we were going to be doing things that others didn't have to do. Those responsibilities were:

1) **Get to know my learning style**

We were given the task of discovering how we learn best. I was given New York Jets' safety Victor Green to study and learn as much about him as I could. I did this through reading old media guides, scouting reports, game summaries, and looking at a ton of tape. Once I was done, I had to put together a report and present it to my offensive coaches. Yes, school was back in session. To become great, you can't just rely on being a great athlete; you have to be a great student at all times.

2) **Chalk Talk**

We would meet with our position coaches three times a week to go through and review the offensive playbooks and schemes for the new system we would be running. Also, we reviewed all the different defenses, including how to read the fronts and coverages, how to adjust pre-snap and how to react on the fly once the play starts.

3) **NFL Europe**

NFL Europe was similar to the farm system for baseball. NFL teams had the option to send players overseas to get more playing time under their belts and develop. I was slated to go to Barcelona and play for the Barcelona Dragons. Yes! When I found this out, I was extremely excited. I would get to travel to Barcelona and pursue my dream further. It doesn't get much better than that.

These additions to my schedule made me excited about the possibilities. I was getting more opportunities to learn and work on my craft.

But what do you think happened?

Smooth sailing from now until training camp, right?

Maybe not?

Turn the page and you'll see.

Mansfield High School

Mom, Brother and Me

UMass Amherst Minutemen

The NFL

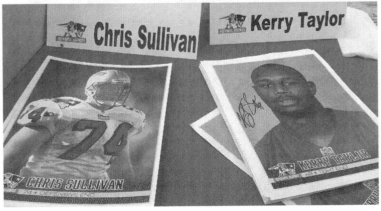

Arena Football

Coaching at Mansfield High School

212 Health and Performance

Proud Dad

Chapter 9
Roll with the Punches

My first NFL off-season was an interesting one. Talk about peaks and valleys, highs and lows! As I mentioned in Chapter 8, my buddies, Marc, Sean and a few other players and myself were slated to go to NFL Europe, more specifically the Barcelona Dragons. So, my focus turned to getting myself ready. YES! YES! The sun, beach, football, Europe, what could be better?

Not so fast, though. It wasn't long before everything came to a screeching halt!

I was towards the end of my workout one day when a passing voice abruptly interrupted the music, "Kerry, please see me after you finish your workout." I stopped what I was doing to chase the voice and put a face with it. It was our Offensive Coordinator, Charlie Weiss.

"Sure, Coach."

Immediately my mind started to race. Up to this point there was no reason for me to go up to his office that I knew of, unless it was to give me my walking papers. I apprehensively completed my workout and headed up to Coach's office. Just before I walked in, the thought of the grim reaper entered my mind. I thought to myself, *they didn't send him for me, so maybe I'm okay.*

I stood outside the door, straightened up my posture, head held high, and then walked into the room. It felt like an eternity before I reached the seat. "Hey, Coach," I said as confidently as I could.

"Kerry, we've been doing some thinking, and we think ("Here it comes," I said to myself as my body tensed up.) you have a strong chance to make the team and contribute next year. So, I think I want to keep you here to learn the offensive system. What do you think?"

"Sure, Coach! Sounds good to me, if you think that's what's best for me to make the team. Let's go for it." Whew! My heart was beating a mile a minute.

And just like that, NFL Europe was no longer in my future. I was staying home in the New England sun. ("New England" and "sun" have probably never been used in a sentence together like that!)

As I write this, I'm having one of those "If I could do it over again" moments. If I could go back to that conversation, I probably would have at least made my case to get to NFL Europe. The slight oversight on my part was the fact that I would have been able to measure myself up against other potential NFL talent, and also get myself on film for the other 31 teams. In the NFL, what you put on tape is everything. It's your resume. *Sigh*. Okay, moment over.

Since I was no longer going to NFL Europe, I had to focus on how I was best going to take advantage of the new opportunity put in front of me. I attended every mini-camp and workout we had that off-season. I figured this would help make sure I would be ready, physically and mentally, for what I was about to embark on, and when training camp arrived, I would be in my best shape possible. Everything was going according to plan until our last mini-camp before training camp. You know when they say, "Only worry about what you can control?" Well, I started to get worried about things I couldn't control, which led to me trying to be too perfect. Yes, you can try to be too perfect, because being perfect doesn't exist. I was just trying too hard, and I couldn't relax. Doing this started to change my style of play, and it wasn't for the better.

Want to know how and why?

Then keep reading, because in the next chapter, I dive a little deeper into what happened at that final mini-camp before training camp started.

CHAPTER 10

The Competition Increases

At this point, I was a ball of stress and worry. Why?

Well, the landscape of our roster and my position was about to change. New guys were being brought in left and right. Anyone who fully and truly follows football knows that when a new coach comes in, he slowly changes the roster and brings his own people in. I was getting nervous because at that time there were three of us when the off-season started—Eric Bjornson, Rod Rutledge and me. They had released Ben Coates, the player I tried to model my game after in high school and college.

Not bad, right? Well, I knew they were going to probably bring in one, maybe two, more guys to the position and let us compete. By the time the last mini-camp started, there were three more guys added to the position—Rob Tardio, Chris Eitzmann, and Dave Stachelski.

Anyone who knows me well knows that I never back down from a competition or a challenge. That wasn't my worry at all. My worry was that my opportunities to show what I could do would decrease drastically. There are only X amount of reps you get in practice. The more people at your position, the more that number gets divided up. Hopefully, the chances I would get would really showcase my talents. God forbid you make a mistake, because that means an opportunity goes down the drain. The key, and what coaches look for, is that you have a short memory when you make a mistake and how you come back from it.

Unfortunately for me, my memory was not short and I couldn't let things go. Instead of me being the hardworking, carefree athlete on the field that was able to showcase his talents, I started to play like a (excuse my language) tight ass that was afraid to make mistakes. That's not how you play the game. It really started to show itself to me when we were doing an open field tackling drill. My goal was to make the tackler miss. However, I couldn't make one person miss because I was moving too much like a robot, too afraid to make a mistake. It got to a point that after practice and films that day, my position coach asked me to have a private conversation. I remember it like it was yesterday.

"Kerry, what's going on? You're not yourself out there."

"I don't know, Coach. But I'll shake it off."

"Listen, I know there are more guys at your position, but that cannot affect how you play. You have a limited amount of snaps and you have to make them count."

"I got it, Coach."

"Listen, if you weren't good enough, you wouldn't be here at all, or have been around all last season. Just relax and play."

"Got it!"

After that conversation, I knew I had to get my sh*t together. That was his or the team's way of saying, "We're watching you and want to know if you're worth keeping around." I got up and went for a two-hour drive to nowhere to collect my thoughts and try to clear my head.

Eventually I was able to relax and regain the confidence in myself and my abilities. I was doing better every day in practice and my position coach confirmed it during film sessions by complimenting some of the plays I was making. But was it too little, too late?

You'll have to keep reading to find out if your boy had what it takes.

CHAPTER 11

The Grim Reaper Reappears

I had my head back on straight and had been performing better up to this point, finishing off our last mini-camp feeling very confident in myself and my abilities. I couldn't wait to strap the pads back on and see what another year of experience, training and learning had done for me.

Beep . . . beep . . . beep . . . beep! The alarm went off at 5 a.m., and I jumped out of bed that morning ready to rock and roll and get training camp started. I left the house in an amazingly great and confident mood. I pulled up to the stadium, waved at the security guy as I drove in on cloud nine. It seemed kind of like those commercials where everything just has you feeling on top of the world. I hopped out of the car and walked down to my locker to put my stuff away. I said hello to a few teammates and headed upstairs to our Training Camp Kickoff Meeting, ready to get this season underway. I hit that top step, took a turn around the corner with a couple of the guys and one of the staff members started small talk with me about training camp.

Then it happened . . .

"Kerry, Coach Belichick would like to see you."

I felt so good and positive that day that I just figured he wanted to have a brief chat with me about their expectations for me. Ha! Who was I kidding? I walked over to the Coach's office, took a seat and it began, yet again!

Coach B: "Kerry, we have six people at your position. Unfortunately, we are only going to bring five into camp. You're the odd man out."

Me: *Really? This sh*t is happening again?* I thought. "Thank you for the opportunity, Coach. Is there anything I could have done better?"

Coach B: "No, you did everything right. You're just the odd man out."

WTF! Give me something! Odd man out? Are you serious?? I had that moment that we all may have had at some point (or maybe it's just me). It's a blackout moment. I envisioned myself getting up and saying my piece and then reality came back. I stood up and said, "Thank you,

Coach," and walked out. I grabbed my stuff from my locker and drove around the rest of the day aimlessly trying to get my thoughts together and search for an answer.

Crazy how a day can start out great and end so disappointing. I finally got myself together and drove home to let my mother know what had happened. I dragged my feet, walked in with my head down, sulking. Not only did I just get released, the dream I had of buying my mom a huge home seemed so far away. I told her the news, and she said in true Donna Taylor fashion, "I know you feel bad right now, but oh, well. Their loss! Keep your head up and get back to work. If you want it to happen, keep working hard to make it happen," while giving me a huge hug.

The first hurdle was over. Now I was going to have to tell people I was released. Man! I didn't leave my house for two weeks because of my disappointment. I felt I had let all the kids down who looked up to me and asked me for my autograph. The one kid I didn't want to disappoint was my younger brother, and I felt like that's what I just did. He looked up to me, and I wanted to lay a path of success for him to follow in life—leave footprints, so to speak.

But as they say, when one door closes, another opens.

Will another door open?

Check out Chapter 12 and see what happens.

Until next time, continue to live life 1° above the rest.

CHAPTER 12
Stay Ready

I s the journey over yet?
Ha ha. Not quite.

Finally, I was able to shake off the disappointment of being released from the New England Patriots, and I got back to work performing my own "two-a-days," if you will. I did early morning running sessions followed up a little later in the day with some hard work in the weight room. I did it with the hope of another call coming in to say, "Kerry, we would like to bring you in."

In the meantime, I set my sights on something I told myself I would always do, give back to my high school— more specifically, the football team. I approached Coach Michael Redding, who started me on my football journey, to see if I could join his staff. If you remember, he was the coach who visited me in Detroit during training camp. Just like that I was back on the playing field, but as an Assistant Coach for the freshman football team. That year was an amazingly fun-filled year for me. I was able to take all I had learned and start to give it back to a very special group of kids. The main goal was to get them to understand that, "If I can do it, so can you." To this day, that year and that group of kids hold, and will always have, a special place in my heart. If you jump to their senior year. I am so proud to say that they ended up graduating as one of the best teams to ever play at Mansfield High School!

The season came to a close and there was no word from my agent that things were looking up, so I started to try and figure out the answer to the question, "Now what?" I looked into starting a career in multiple areas:

- High School Teacher

- Liquor Sales Representative

- Beverage Sales Representative

- Financial Advisor

- College Football Coach

- Insurance Salesman

- College Strength and Conditioning Coach

I went on many interviews and researched more areas that I thought would work for me. One day, I came home from an interview at Fidelity. There was a message on my note pad left for me that said, "Call back." They didn't leave a message but expressed that it was important. I called back, figuring it was one of the companies that I interviewed with, but lo and behold, I was not done yet! There was a little life breathed back into my pro football career. The message was from one of the coaches that was a part of the newly-formed XFL. This league was going to be run by the WWF and Vince McMahon.

Yes! This was the opportunity I was looking for and another chance to showcase my skills. With luck, I might even get back into the NFL. I went for it and signed a contract to play for the L.A. Xtreme. This league was going to be different than the eleven-on-eleven game you and I knew, but it was football. The dial of training was turned up to another level to prepare for what was to come.

Would this lead me back to the NFL or would I just become a guy who played in the XFL for a few years?

As always, you will need to keep reading to find out.

Continue to live a life 1° above the rest!

CHAPTER 13

Quit or Keep Pushing?

G reat! You're not sick of my story yet, and I didn't lose you. Thanks for making it this far.

My football story was not quite done yet. As you learned in the last chapter, I came back home from an interview and there was a message from a coach at the XFL. That's when I packed my bags and headed out west to play for the L.A. Xtreme.

The XFL was a fun time—an interesting league and brand of football. It was like you threw the NFL, CFL, AFL, and WWE into a bowl, mixed it up with a bunch of high-level football players, coaches, baked it, and out came the XFL. For those who aren't aware, some of the glaring differences were:

- A player can go in motion anywhere, not just side to side like the NFL, or forward and back like the CFL and AFL.

- Instead of a regular old coin toss, it was a 40-yard dash. The person who gets the ball when the whistle blows wins the coin toss.

- The television cameras were everywhere, on the field, in the huddle, in the stands.

- The Super Bowl was called the Million Dollar Game where the winning team splits $1 million.

- You could put any name you wanted on the back of your jersey.

- No fair catches.

With all these differences, it was still football. It's just that the presentation wasn't always the best. It was very rushed to get the product on the field. We had a short training camp and then the season started. All in all, as a player, it was a great time, despite what critics say.

When the season concluded, I didn't have any calls from an NFL team. What I hoped for, an opportunity to get back in the NFL, never came to fruition, so I just planned to return to the XFL the following season. Of course, shortly after that, I received a phone call that the XFL season had been cancelled.

Well, there goes that idea. So, my focus then shifted again. I said to myself, "Self, here we go again. Time to start looking for another career." All the while, in the back of my mind, I was hoping for another break to get a chance to get back on the field. I stayed with my workout routine of two-a-days, doing workouts in the early morning and in the afternoon.

I did drag my feet for a while when it came to looking for a job. I didn't put my whole self in it because it was like I was giving up on myself. I was giving up on a dream. Eventually, taking the advice of my old college strength coach and mentor, Bob Otrando, I became a Personal Trainer and continued as a High School Football Coach. It was a marriage made in heaven for me. I loved both opportunities. I was able to take so many aspects of my life and apply them into both jobs. The hard work, overcoming adversity, learning, teaching, leading, motivating . . . man, I'm getting excited just thinking about my early years of coaching from both aspects.

As the high school football season was underway and my clientele list rapidly grew, guess what happened?

You guessed it.

Another phone call, but from a league I had never heard of, the Arena Football League. What was this all about? I had no idea. All I knew is that it was indoors. But again, it was not the type of football I was used to. But your boy was charged up, excited and ready to see what it was all about!

As you continue reading, you will see how I made my transition from eleven-on-eleven outdoor football to eight-on-eight indoor, fan-friendly football.

Until next time, live life 1° above the rest.

CHAPTER 14

Let's Take it Inside

Here I was, on my way to embark on another possible football adventure. The call came from a coach from the Dallas Desperados, which was a new team in the Arena Football League. I was asked if I would come down for a tryout. I had to fly out the following week to see if I had what it took to be a part of their team. Thankfully, I had been working out, doing drills and being around football, so I was ready to go at a drop of a hat.

When I finally got there, I was a nervous wreck. But I was definitely ready to go. (Side note: high school football fields in Texas make some college fields look like a playground!)

When we finally got to our destination, tryouts began. The testing and all the general drills went well, but then it was time to do drills more specific to the Arena game. I felt I did okay but could've done better. When it was all said and done, we were pulled into a group meeting and told, "A coach will meet with you back at the hotel before you leave to let you know what's going on."

When I got back to my room and was about to have a bite to eat, my hotel room phone rang. It was Coach Norris on the other end asking to meet him in the lobby where I would learn my fate. We spoke for about twenty minutes on how the day went and some of the things he felt I could work on. At the end was an invite to training camp to try to make the Dallas Desperados Arena Football Team.

YES! (Insert Tiger Woods Fist pump here!)

So, what is Arena football?

Here's a quick synopsis of it before I go any further, for those who aren't familiar with Arena ball.

The Arena Football League is a professional indoor football league. It was founded in 1987 by Jim Foster, who came up with the idea watching an indoor soccer game. While at the game, he wrote the idea on an envelope with different sketches and notes. The goal was to create a game that was similar to outdoor football, but faster paced, higher scoring, fan-friendly and encouraged offensive performance.

Defensive Specialists: This player is designated every game and plays just defense, usually a defensive back.

Offensive Specialists: This player plays just offense (besides the QB), usually a receiver.

Motions: Can happen in every direction.

Substitutions: The starter can have a sub, but once the sub comes in and goes out, he cannot come back in for the current quarter.

All kicks are live, no punting: If you miss a field goal, it's a live ball and can be returned.

The box: The linebackers can only run in the area, five yards away from the line of scrimmage and in between the tackles, hence the name "area box."

Fan-friendly: If the ball goes in the stands you keep the ball, players can go over the boards and end up in your lap.

Iron Man football: everyone plays both ways except for the specialists and the QB.

Another league, another set of rules, another set of coaches, another opportunity to prove myself.

Stay tuned to find out what happens.

Until then, continue to live life 1° above the rest.

CHAPTER 15
Can't Make the Club in the Tub

As you just learned, the final whistle had not been blown on my career. My next pursuit to keep it going was heading into Arena Football and seeing what that might lead to. A lot of guys had gone on to play Arena Football and were able to get back into an NFL training camp.

Hmm . . . we'll see.

The Arena game is a fun game to play and watch. As a player, you're taking it back to Iron Man Football. I played fullback and linebacker which, in my opinion, are the toughest positions to play in the Arena game. You basically are doing the same thing on both sides of the ball. One side, you're attacking and trying to destroy your opponent, and on the other side, you're playing guardian and protecting the QB. Ninety percent of the time it was a car crash that you knew was coming and had to do your best to make sure you could get into another accident!

At this time, the game was completely new to me, but I loved every bit of it. It was a lot quicker than the eleven-man game we all know so well. As training camp started with the Dallas Desperados, it took a while to get used to the differences in the game, and I caught myself thinking way too much. Any athlete who understands sports will tell you, the more you're out there thinking, the less you can be yourself and the athlete you want to be. The true "you" doesn't come out until things can happen naturally. For that very reason, I was struggling to shine like I wanted to, but I knew, deep down inside, that once I was comfortable, I would be okay. I just hoped it would happen before it was too late.

Every practice and film study, I was becoming increasingly more comfortable with the game. Then, the most frustrating thing that could happen to any football player, especially those trying to make a team, happened.

Do you know what it is?

Arghh . . . yeah, you guessed it.

The injury bug bit me in practice while blitzing and having one of our normal collisions. I had my head down too much and ended up spraining my neck. The saying is,

"You can't make the club in the tub." So now I was regulated to playbook, film study and mental reps.

UGH! Now what?

The neck isn't something you push through, so I rested it and rehabbed as much as possible until I received the A-OK from the doc. When I was finally cleared, it was time to make a statement of what I could do. Practices went well. I didn't have any of the nervousness you think you would have after injuring your neck. Before long, it was time to play a real game.

I played a bit and thought I played well enough, but a week later I was released and heading back home again. Frustrated and pissed off, I truly felt that except for the neck injury, I would've been on that team through the whole season. So, home I went to get myself 100% healthy and wait for, hopefully, another call to play somewhere. I was back to being a trainer and coach.

Eventually, the phone did ring again, and it was the New Haven Ninjas, which was an Arena 2 Football Team in Connecticut. Being a part of this team was going to be tougher to manage than it was in the past with other teams. Any idea why?

Keep reading, and as always, continue to live life 1° above the rest.

CHAPTER 16

Time to Take a Step Back and Regroup

In the last chapters, you learned that my journey as a pro football player had taken me into the Arena Football league. My journey there had almost ended due to a neck injury but, by the grace of the football gods, they decided to give me another chance. Arena 2 Football, here I come!

Arena 2 Football was essentially a farm system for Arena 1 football, so I was going to be able to learn the game and prove I have what it takes to play at the next level of Arena Football. It was an opportunity to hone my craft and skills at this level and get over the neck injury. It also gave me time to build up my confidence that I could create and take on collisions with no problem.

Being a part of this team had a unique twist to it. One twist is that the pay was significantly less than what I was getting paid in the NFL, XFL and at the Arena 1 Level, so with that being said, money became an issue. All of us had to continue to do our full- or part-time jobs and balance playing at the same time. We only practiced once a week and played our games over the weekend. Let me give you the picture how this worked for me.

My daily work schedule looked like this:

Wake up: 4 a.m.

Clients: 5 a.m.-12 p.m.

Workout: 12 p.m.-1:30 p.m.

Break: 1:30 p.m.-4 p.m.

Clients: 4 p.m.-8 p.m.

That was my daily schedule for the most part, plus the weekends. How the hell was I going to fit football practice and games into this schedule? New Haven is in Connecticut, which was a two-hour drive itself. I had no idea, but I was determined to figure it out. So, I adjusted some things around and thankfully, I had clients who were willing to adjust their schedule to continue to work with me. Now my schedule was going to look like this over the next three-four months:

Monday, Tuesday, Thursday

    Wake up: 4 a.m.

    Clients: 5 a.m.-12 p.m.

    Workout: 12 p.m.-1:30 p.m.

    Break: 1:30 p.m.-4 p.m.

    Clients: 4 p.m.-9 p.m.

Wednesday

    Wake up: 4 a.m.

    Clients: 5 a.m.-12 p.m.

    Workout: 12 p.m.-2 p.m.

    Break: 2 p.m.-4 p.m.

Practice plus travel time: 4 p.m.-12 a.m.

Friday & Saturday

    Wake: 4 a.m.

    Clients: 5 a.m.-12 p.m.

Travel to Connecticut to catch the bus for the game (if away game).

Sunday

    Work or rest day, depending on clients

Yes, it was tough road to travel but I wouldn't have had it any other way. If you want something badly enough, you fight for it, and fight for it, I did. As a matter of fact, all of us did, and that is what made our team a tight team. We were all making sacrifices to play this game we loved, and some used this as a stepping-stone to get to the next level of football.

Our first season together as a team was a great one. We made it to the playoffs. Unfortunately, I could not participate after having a great season because, well, with two minutes to go in the game leading into the playoffs, our opponent was on the comeback trail and kicked an onside kick. I was blindsided by someone and silence fell across the stadium. I was staring at the ceiling, saying to myself, "I'm going to get this guy back on the next play," and some other choice words I won't share here. But I couldn't get up, my leg wouldn't cooperate. As I continued to struggle to get back on my feet, a teammate rushed over to me and held me down.

"Kerry, don't get up and don't look down," my teammate and friend, Anthony, said as he gestured over to the sideline that someone hurry up and get out here. A few coaches and a doctor rushed onto the field. I still had no idea what was going on. My adrenaline was running so high that I couldn't feel any pain, not until the doctor told me what happened that is.

"Kerry, you dislocated your hip."

With lightning speed, pain took over my lower half which was nothing compared to what they were about to do. Yes, you guessed, they were going to put it back in the socket on the field. A deafening silence overtook the stadium as the doctor and coaches attempted to get my femur back into my hip socket. They tugged at it three times, unsuccessfully. I mean, I wasn't helping any. Every time they pulled, I jumped to punch someone to let go of my leg. With each tug, I let out a huge blood-curdling scream. On the fourth attempt to fix me up, the doctor said, "Okay, this time we are going to do it on three. Ready? One . . ." I continued with "2," but at that moment the doctor yanked and put it back into place like magic before I could figure out what was going on. Fourth time's the charm, ha ha. Yeah, I'm not bullshitting you—another injury setback. I was regulated to cheering my team on. Unfortunately, we were ousted out of the playoffs after the first round.

Now what?

I had moved from the NFL to XFL to Arena Football to Arena 2. Don't get me wrong. Arena 2 Ball was a great time, but that ended with a dislocated hip. And it was the worst pain ever, by the way!

Sheesh, where do I turn now?

Like most athletes, you get back on your horse and work to get yourself back in order. It wasn't that hard physically, but mentally, it was a tough thing to overcome. As I started to make great progress in my training, the phones rang. It was the New York Dragons Arena 1 Football Team. They wanted to bring me in for a workout. Talk about motivation to really get back in order. I stepped my game up in the weight room, running on the track and even added yoga into my training two days a week.

When the day came, I was physically ready to knock it out of the park. I performed well enough for them to sign me and bring me into camp. I eventually made the team and continued my football career there, and then ended up going to the Arizona Rattlers and enjoyed my time out there.

Unfortunately, some things happened in the organization that made me start to question if I wanted to pursue this anymore. After long talks with close friends, I decided to walk away from the sport that gave me so much. I met some of my closest friends and found some of my mentors in life. I traveled the country, did and saw things that I could only dream of. It was a painful decision and not an easy one to make. If things had happened differently, I probably would have continued to play, but my path is my path. It has been full of twists and turns, ups and downs and everything in between.

Trying to get to the highest level in a game you love is never easy, but if you want to make it happen, you must always go for it. It may come right away, or it may take a while, but you will benefit either way.

So, go for it!

CHAPTER 17
The Rear View

Wow! Thank you for taking the time to read this book about my journey to try and reach the Mount Everest of football. I know there have been many others who embarked on a journey like this, but this was my personal one. This one was Taylor Made.

Every experience I had along the way has helped me to become the man I am today. I now share those thoughts and lessons in some form with the athletes I coach and clients I work with every day at 212. Through this book, I am sharing them with you as well. What these lessons teach you is that "YOU CAN" make it happen. I hope you recognize that my journey runs parallel with what you are trying to achieve in life or in fitness. Nothing worthwhile in life comes easily or without a cost. It first starts with a dream in your head. From there, you will be challenged and face adversity. The real question is, what will you do when it pops up? Will you back down or continue to push?

Some of the themes that run true in my life and my journey:

* **Never give up on yourself if it's important to you.**

* **Life is full of peaks and valleys. Do your best to not hang in the valleys too long and learn from your journeys down in the valley.**

* **Give your best effort every day.**

* **A little encouragement can go a long way**

* **When things don't go your way, shake it off and learn from it.**

* **Take a step towards what you want every day. Whether it is a big step or small, you're still going in the right direction.**

* **Change is inevitable. How are you going to deal with it moving forward?**

* **There will be those in life who believe in you and others who don't. Let the doubters fuel your engine to succeed.**

* **Even if you fail, it doesn't mean you're a failure.**

* **Competition can bring out the best of you, but also the worst.**

* **Leave it all out there, and don't have regrets.**

* **Be in the moment.**

* **Enjoy your successes. Don't be so quick to let them go.**

* **Get 1° better every day. If you do that, imagine where you will be at the end of a week, a month or a year.**

* **The biggest battle is to just "Show Up;" if you can just show up, you have the average person beat every day. Most people are afraid to just "Show Up."**

My message to anyone out there who thinks they want to play professional football, or any other sport is, "Go for it and give it your all. If you're not willing to give it your all, don't bother." Being great at sports, or anything at all, takes time and dedication, not just on the field but off the field as well. Everything you do affects your outcome. Just know that the journey is always worth it because of the people you meet and the lessons you learn. The lessons are your golden nuggets. Always search for them. You may not know it in the moment, but when you have a chance to look back at it all, you will start to understand and be able to connect the dots. Hard work, dedication, and sacrifice are not easy things to come by and deliver on. Many people are great at giving you lip service and tell you they have what it takes or will do what it takes, but they really can't bring themselves to that level. Can you?

My experience in the NFL meant the world to me. Here I was, a skinny inner-city kid who never once thought he could play professional sports. I shaped and molded myself to be the best version of me that I could be. I mean, come on, how many kids can say they made it to that level? Real life statistics at the time of publishing this book state that 0.0009% of high school football players get drafted and play in the NFL. I was one of the very few. I didn't fully enjoy myself when I got there because I was so focused on what was next. I wish I had taken a little time to realize that what I accomplished was so rare and hard to do. It's hard to get there, even harder to make a team and stick around. This all means and proves to me that you can achieve anything that you want through hard work, sacrifice and commitment. It's always rewarded. Maybe not in the way you want it to at the current time, but it's always rewarded, it just may show up later in life.

Being released by the Patriots and suffering that huge disappointment was difficult and a challenging thing to handle mentally. But it also taught me a lot about myself. I will get knocked down, but I will fight like hell to get back up and continue to move forward. Remember that when you are faced with challenges and disappointments in your own life, it will never be smooth sailing. Are you going to let it win, or are you going to fight to get back up and make your life what you want it to be? Everything is in your hands. The choice is truly yours.

Acknowledgements

It's a challenging and difficult decision to put your pen to paper and put yourself out there for the world to see and judge. However, if you don't take a shot and do it anyway, you will never know what's possible. Thank you to those along this journey who helped me bring this book to life and who always gave me the courage in life to go for it and step out on faith! Thank you!

Special thanks go out to:

Mom, I didn't always have everything, but you always found a way to make sure Blayne and I had what we needed to succeed in life.

Adrionna, my amazing daughter for unknowingly pushing me to be better in every aspect of my life, teaching me how to be present and enjoy the special things in life. Daddy loves you, baby!

Ashley, for all your advice as I put this all together including your contributions of helping me work through the title and taking the photo for the cover. Most of all, thank you for always believing in me and having my back, no matter what!

Marc Megna, my good friend and teammate. Thank you for your battles on the field, motivation and drive off the field in the gym and in life and most of all, for your friendship. Thank you for your contribution to this project by writing the Foreword. I'm extremely grateful!

Coach Bob Otrando, for turning this athletic skinny freshman into one of the stronger athletes to pass through the UMass Football Program, teaching me the ins and outs of the weight room and what a great strength and conditioning program looks like. I carry those lessons with me to this day.

My **'98 National Championship Team** for showing ourselves and countless others that anything is possible with hard work and a joint commitment to a common goal! What we achieved will never be achieved again.

Coach Hodges, you took a chance on me and allowed me to play at the next level. I wasn't sure if I belonged early on, but that quickly changed over time. I'm forever grateful for the opportunity that you gave me to succeed. It changed the course of my life!

Coach Whipple and **Coach Christ**, thank you for bringing out all of my athletic talents and displaying them on the football field. It allowed me to go on this entire journey.

Heather, one of my dearest friends and the glue of 212. Thank you for always challenging me, keeping me on my toes, being by my side and reminding me that, "I'm Kerry F-in Taylor. LOL!"

Tracy and Nick Rabar, for sharing your experience and journey of writing a book. "A-Team!"

To all the athletes and clients, I've had the opportunity to coach and hopefully, impacted your lives in a positive way, because you've all impacted mine.

My 212 Team, for making 212 an amazing community that people come to, to make their lives 1 degree better everyday.

Kelli and **Greg** and the whole Scriptor Publishing crew for sticking by me and coaching me through this process even though I wanted to back out more than once. When I didn't have the confidence to write a book, you kept me on track and smacked some sense into me when needed. Thank you for pushing me to be uncomfortable.

Coach Redding and the rest of the coaches at Mansfield High School, thank you for seeing something in the new kid in town when I may have not seen it in myself.

And finally, to the few friends out there who encouraged me and challenged me to take this step and told me I should put myself out there. Follow my example and get a little uncomfortable. If not, you may never know what you can achieve. It's where the magic happens.

Made in the USA
Lexington, KY
05 November 2019

56574826R00066